Multicultural Folk Dance
Guide

Volume 2

Christy Lane
Susan Langhout

Human Kinetics

Library of Congress Cataloging-in-Publication Data

Lane, Christy.
    Multicultural folk dance guide / Christy Lane, Susan Langhout.
       p.   cm.
    ISBN 0-88011-905-5 (v. 1). -- ISBN 0-88011-921-7 (v. 2)
    1. Folk dancing.   2. Manners and customs.   3. Folk dancing--Study
and teaching.   I. Langhout, Susan, 1966- . II. Title.
GV1743.L36   1998
793.3'1--dc21   98-10648
                                                    CIP

ISBN: 0-88011-921-7

Developmental Editor: Judy Patterson Wright, PhD; **Managing Editors:** Lynn M. Hooper-Davenport and Lisa Satterthwaite; **Graphic Designer:** Nancy Rasmus; **Graphic Artists:** Sandra Meier and Francine Hamerski; **Cover Designer:** Jack Davis; **Printer:** United Graphics

Printed in the United States of America   10 9 8 7 6

Human Kinetics
Web site: www.HumanKinetics.com

United States: Human Kinetics
P.O. Box 5076
Champaign, IL 61825-5076
800-747-4457
e-mail: humank@hkusa.com

Canada: Human Kinetics
475 Devonshire Road, Unit 100
Windsor, ON N8Y 2L5
800-465-7301 (in Canada only)
e-mail: orders@hkcanada.com

Europe: Human Kinetics
107 Bradford Road
Stanningley
Leeds LS28 6AT, United Kingdom
+44 (0)113 255 5665
e-mail: hk@hkeurope.com

Australia: Human Kinetics
57A Price Avenue
Lower Mitcham, South Australia 5062
08 8277 1555
e-mail: liaw@hkaustralia.com

New Zealand: Human Kinetics
Division of Sports Distributors NZ Ltd.
P.O. Box 300 226 Albany
North Shore City, Auckland
0064 9 448 1207
e-mail: blairc@hknewz.com

The *Multicultural Folk Dance Treasure Chest* (including the booklet, music, and video packages) is dedicated to all the young people in the world. It is hoped that all the diverse cultures that make up this vast and exciting place we live in will be brought together with a better understanding of each other through dance, thus increasing peace and harmony.

CONTENTS

ACKNOWLEDGMENTS

I am grateful to the following individuals who have contributed to this project. First, I would like to acknowledge Rainer Martens for his ability to see the importance of dance in our society and for his insight, vision, and willingness to help young people around the world. My gratitude is extended to Richard Duree, dance ethnologist and historian, for consulting on this project. Sincere thanks to Adrienne Sabo, Margaret Roza, Lynnanne Hanson, Charlie Griswold, Pete and Portia Seanoa, Judith Scalin, Louise Reichlin, Bob Osgood, Elaine Weisman, Char Schade, Jerry Krause, David Rojas, Scot Byars, Francesco Geora, Derrick J. LaSalla, Carlos Vigon, Loyola Marymount University dance department, University of Southern California dance department, City of Los Angeles Cultural Affairs, Aman Folk Ensemble, Highland School District in Burien, Washington, National Dance Association, Westchester Lariats, and all the dancers and teachers who participated in the creation of the *Multicultural Folk Dance Treasure Chest,* for their time, advice, and support of this project. It was a pleasure to work with such a great production team, especially Doug Fink, Roger Francisco, Bobby Morganstein, Rick Hall, Studio West, Mr. Scenic, Snap Lock Company, and the incredible staff at Human Kinetics. Finally, my most sincere appreciation is extended to all the teachers I have met around the country for their inspiration, optimism, and desire to share dance.

Christy Lane

INTRODUCTION

Welcome to the wonderful world of dance! You are about to experience folk dancing, the oldest form of dance. It is the basis for many other dance forms. The term *folk dancing* is usually defined as "the dance of the common people." Just where or when it began is impossible to document. Archaeologists and historians say it was a basic part of early peoples' culture as they used dance to communicate their emotions through movement and rhythm. People have danced and still dance for celebration, for survival, to socialize, to communicate with the spiritual, and to express their membership and identity in communities.

The purpose of this combined video, music, and booklet package is to provide simplified, hands-on tools for those wishing to participate in a meaningful and enjoyable program of folk dance. On the video, each dance is taught by an expert or a native of the country from which the dance originates. The dances have been carefully chosen to provide a successful and meaningful experience to all involved and an optimal mix of cultural diversity and samples for different levels. The dances selected were a result of a nationwide survey. Each dance has appropriate musical accompaniment that was specifically developed for use with the videotape and this booklet. The music was derived from original, authentic compositions of the popular songs used with the selected dances.

Folk Dancing Benefits

This volume gives you an opportunity to learn about nine cultures. Each dance reflects the geography, climate, music, lifestyles, beliefs, and history of a people. It takes on the characteristics of the locale. For example, climate is a factor of great importance. Generally, the dances from frigid climates are quick-moving with strong, vigorous movements and sustained action. Dances from very warm climates have fluid movements and are more flowing and slow. In temperate climates, the dances seem to be more balanced between the vigorous and quiet actions. Mountain dwellers tend to be more isolated and less mobile than those who live in the plains, and their dances tend to be done in one place, while the dances of the people of the plains fly across the floor as though the dancers were riding horseback across the great open plains.

The forms, patterns, and functions of folk dance vary as much as the cultures. The dances can be done with or without partners; in circles, squares, or long lines; in threesomes, foursomes, or alone. As a means of expression, dances such as wedding dances, war dances, contest dances, courtship dances, work dances, religious dances, and special holiday dances have been created.

Folk dancing is very social and recreational in nature. Each dancer is a member of a larger group, and dancers change partners frequently during many of the dances, promoting communication between people who might otherwise be too timid. Folk dancing helps to develop rhythmic movements, neuromuscular coordination, balance, and poise. It is a challenge to learn new skills, and dance allows participants, regardless of their ages, the satisfaction of both achievement and acceptance.

How to Use This Booklet

In this guide, you will find the following information for each of the nine dances:

- Origin
- Location
- Language
- Flag
- Traditional costume
- History
- Difficulty level
- Stance
- Music selection and time signature
- Number of participants
- Formation
- Directions
- Modifications
- Trivia

Selected photographs taken from the video illustrate portions of the dance and show the dancers in action. As appropriate, a diagram is included to show the formation of the dance. You may use the modification suggestions either to simplify the dance or to add variety. The nine dances in this volme are presented in easy-to-difficult order and reflect three degrees of difficulty—easy, moderate, and advanced. The easy dances are shorter and less complex than the advanced dances, which have more intricate steps performed to a faster tempo. Each dance concludes with an interesting bit of trivia to enhance your understanding of the culture.

If you are a teacher, you'll find the For Teachers Only section to be helpful. It includes suggestions for presenting, managing, and introducing dances in order to keep things fun and interesting for all. Lastly, there is a Resources section that identifies the selected dance instructors and lists equipment sources.

Authentic music and rhythm are important in all folk dances. Rhythm is the beat that drives dance movements. It is the musical sound that catches the essential style and quality of the dance. Time signatures of 2/4, 3/4, 4/4, and 6/8 are commonly used in Western cultures. Eastern cultures tend to use irregular meters such as 5/16, 7/8, and 11/16. Both the specific music selection and the time signature are listed per dance. Also, see page 49 of this guide for more information on the companion music and videos available for each volume of dances.

The folk dance experience involves more than performing the steps correctly. It is an opportunity to develop a better understanding of the customs and traditions of other cultures through a nonjudgmental curiosity, and to discover that dance can be a common bond between people of all nations. Folk dance is an expression of the human spirit.

Welcome to an exciting adventure of dance!

Diagram Key

○ = women   □ = men

SYRTOS

(seer-toh')

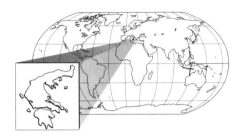

▶ Origin

Greece

▶ Location

Southeastern Europe, bordering the Aegean, Ionian, and Mediterranean Seas

▶ Language

Greek is the official language, but French and English are prevalent also.

▶ Flag

Nine equal horizontal stripes of blue alternating with white. There is a blue square in the upper-left corner with a white cross through it.

▶ Traditional Costume

The man wears a short tunic, pleated white skirt, knee-high stockings, open-neck shirt and trimmed vest, and a long tie belt with tassels hanging down. The woman wears an ankle-length dress, ornamented tunic coat, decorated apron, and colorful scarf with coins on it.

▶ History of Dance

Syrtos is the most popular of all the Greek dances. The basic step is simple enough that anyone can participate. The leader, who is at the right end of the line, dances intricate variations while the line keeps the basic step going. Sometimes a scarf is held between the leader and the second dancer in line to give the leader more flexibility and movement. *Syrtos* translates as "pull or lead," which is the characteristic of the dance.

▶ Difficulty Level
Easy

▶ Stance
Dignified

▶ Music Selection & Time Signature
Gerakina/Samiotisa (7/8 time; often simplified to 2/4)

▶ Number of Participants
No limit; however, it is recommended not to exceed twelve.

▶ Formation
Broken circle, hands joined in a "w" formation at shoulder height.

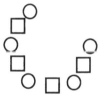

Directions

Note: Begin facing clockwise and on a slight diagonal to the right side. This dance uses a total of 12 weight changes (that is, transferring weight from one foot to the other on the "slow" and the "quick" rhythms listed in the following directions).

Part 1: Eight Walks

(2 counts) Step to the right side onto the right foot and hold (slow).

(2 counts) Continue walking with the left foot, then the right foot (quick, quick).

(2 counts) Step onto the left foot and hold (slow).

(2 counts) Continue walking with the right foot, then the left foot (quick, quick).

(2 counts) Step onto the right foot and hold (slow).

(1 count) Step onto the left foot, placing it in front of the right foot (quick).

Part 2: Back, Side, Cross, Back

(1 count) Step backward (in place) onto the right foot (quick).

(2 counts) Step toward the left side onto the left foot (slow).

(1 count) Step on the right foot placed in front of (crossing) the left foot (quick).

(1 count) Step backward (in place) onto the left foot (quick),

Repeat the entire sequence until the music ends.

▶ Modifications

- Begin at a slow tempo and gradually increase speed.
- Call the dance by counting the number of steps taken, using a rhythm: "1, 2-3, 4, 5-6, 7, 8-9, 10, 11-12," or by saying "slow, quick-quick, slow, quick-quick, slow, quick-quick, slow, quick-quick."
- Try adding a clockwise turn on count 4.

- For the last two quicks (steps 11 and 12), the leader may turn counterclockwise under the arm of the next person in line.
- Change leaders while dancing by letting go of hands and finding a new position.

▶ TRIVIA TIDBITS ◀

- The first Olympics were held in ancient Greece.
- Popular Greek foods include avgolemono (egg-lemon soup), moussaka (eggplant casserole), souvlakia (skewered meat), and baklava (nut-filled pastry dessert).

TANKO BUSHI
(tahn-ko boo'-shè)

 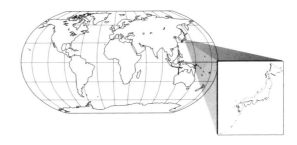

▶ Origin
Japan

▶ Location
Eastern Asia, between the Pacific Ocean and the Sea of Japan

▶ Language
Japanese

▶ Flag
White with a large solid red circle in the center

▶ Traditional Costume
Men and women both wear the *kimono*—a loose robe fastened with a wide sash—and flat wooden shoes.

▶ History of Dance
This dance is approximately 100 years old and is a storytelling dance about the coal miners in Japan. The actions pantomime digging for coal, shoveling it into a cart, shading eyes from the sun, and pushing the coal cart away up a hill. It is performed during summer festivals.

▶ Difficulty Level
Easy

▶ Stance
As a worker digging in the mines

▶ Music Selection & Time Signature
Tanko Bushi (2/4 time)

▶ Number of Participants
No limit

▶ Formation
Single circle facing counterclockwise

Directions

Part 1: Dig and Wipe Your Sweat

(4 counts) Tap the ball of the right foot, then step onto the right foot while pretending to dig twice to the right with a big shovel.

(4 counts) Tap the ball of the left foot, then step onto the left foot while pretending to dig twice to the left with a big shovel.

(2 counts) Step forward on the right foot as you bring your hands together with palms up and pretend to throw coal over your right shoulder.

(2 counts) Step forward on the left foot as you bring your hands together with palms up and pretend to throw coal over your left shoulder.

(2 counts) Rock weight backward to step on the left foot and pretend to shade your eyes or wipe the sweat away with the right hand as the left arm is extended to the side (see photo next page).

(2 counts) Rock weight backward to step on the right foot and pretend to shade your eyes or wipe the sweat away with the left hand as the right arm is extended to the side.

Part 2: Push Cart Forward

(4 counts) Step forward onto the right foot, then step onto the left foot while putting your hands together with palms forward and pretending to push the cart forward twice.

(4 counts) Step forward onto the right foot while bringing your arms to the sides, making a circle, and clap. Step backward onto the left foot, then step backward with the right foot to bring feet together.

(4 counts) Clap . . . pause . . . clap-clap, clap.

Repeat the entire sequence until the music ends.

▶ Modifications

- To simplify, eliminate the footwork and do only the arms.
- Practice dancing in a straight line before attempting a circle.

▶ TRIVIA TIDBITS ◀

- More than 40 percent of the cultivated land in Japan is devoted to rice production.
- Traditional Japanese theater is called *Kabuki*. Kabuki plays and dances may be about grand historical events or the everyday lives of people in the 17th century.

LES SALUTS
(lay sah-lóo)

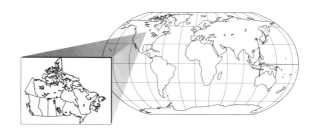

▶ Origin
Canada

▶ Location
North America, on the northern border of the United States, bounded by the Atlantic and Pacific Oceans. This dance originated in the eastern part of Canada in a province called Quebec.

▶ Language
English and French are both official languages.

▶ Flag
Three vertical bands of red, white, and red, with a red maple leaf centered in the white band

▶ Traditional Costume
Men wear pants and shirt with multicolored (red, yellow, blue, green, and black) *flechee* (sashes). Women wear blouses, skirts, and aprons, and may wear straw bonnets.

▶ History of the Dance
One of the forms of social dance in French Canada is the quadrille. The quadrille is related to the American square dance; however, it is not restricted to only four couples in a square formation. Les Saluts is actually one part of a much longer dance called Le Saratoga. Le Saratoga is still performed today on Orleans Island near Quebec City.

▶ Difficulty Level
Easy/moderate

▶ Stance
Upright and dignified

▶ Music Selection & Time Signature
Les Saluts (6/8 time)

▶ Number of Participants
No limit of couples

▶ Formation
Requires a partner. Double circle: Inner circle of women holding hands and outer circle of men holding hands. Partners are close to each other with the woman on the man's right side.

Directions

Part 1: Circle to Side

(8 counts) Women face diagonal left and perform eight walking steps to the left (moving clockwise), while the men face diagonal right and perform eight walking steps to the right (moving counterclockwise).

(8 counts) Repeat above in the opposite direction. The group should end up exactly at their starting positions.

Part 2: Front Basket Figure

(8 counts) The men face the center on the first two counts, raise their joined hands over the women's heads, and lower their arms in front of the women to form a "front basket figure" while stepping forward onto the right foot, then bringing feet together. Simultaneously, the

women bend at the waist (to duck under), take a step backward onto the left foot, then bring feet together. In this new position, everyone walks clockwise forward for six steps.

(8 counts) Continuing in the basket position, everyone walks counter-clockwise for eight steps.

Part 3: Walk Into Center and Out

(4 counts) With arms still crossed, all face the center and walk forward four steps.

(4 counts) Change hand holds to bring hands down at sides of the body as all walk backward four steps to end up in one large circle.

(4 counts) All walk three steps toward the center and slowly take a low bow (wait for the music).

(4 counts) As the music starts again at a faster tempo, men walk four steps backward and join hands as women join hands in an inner circle (return to the starting position).

Dance repeats from the beginning until the end of the music.

▶ Modifications

- In one circle, practice walking both clockwise and counterclockwise, eight counts counterclockwise, then eight counts clockwise, before teaching the dance.
- Omit the "front basket figure" (Part 2), and repeat Part 1 twice.

▶ TRIVIA TIDBITS ◀

- Canada is an Indian word meaning "big village."
- Canada contains more lakes and inland waters than any other country in the world.

TARANTELLA
(tar'-ahn-tel'-a)

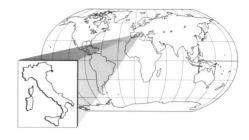

▶ Origin
Italy

▶ Location
Southern Europe: a boot-shaped peninsula extending into the Mediterranean Sea

▶ Language
Italian

▶ Flag
Three equal vertical stripes of green, white, and red

▶ Traditional Costume
Men wear close-fitting, knee-length pants with buttons near the bottom, white shirts with ties at the neck, long sashes wrapped around the waist, and short, decorative jackets. Women wear long-sleeved, below-the-knee dresses with patterned aprons tied at the waist.

▶ History of Dance
The tarantella is an animated dance dealing with the bite of the tarantula spider. It is very lively and fun with lots of pantomime. This version of the popular tarantella dance is based on Sicilian steps. The steps can be mixed and matched to form numerous combinations. A tambourine is optional (see the Resources section at the end of this guide).

▶ Difficulty Level
Moderate

▶ Stance
Upright

▶ Music Selection & Time Signature
Tarantella (6/8 time)

▶ Number of Participants
No limit

▶ Formation
Partners facing each other

Directions

Part 1: Face Front

a. Cross, Cross, Out, Out

(2 counts) Cross the right foot in front of the left, cross the left foot in front of the right.

(2 counts) Step the right foot out to the right side, step the left foot out to the left side.

(4 counts) Repeat the first 4 counts and make a circle with the tambourine clockwise across the body.

(8 counts) Repeat (a).

b. Tarantella Steps

(2 counts) Kick the right foot forward and low to the ground, step on the right foot (slightly crossing in front of the left foot), push against the floor with the ball of the left foot, and step with the right foot again in place, keeping hands on hips. The tarantella step can also be called a *modified triple* step, as a small kick is added, then three weight changes are taken within two beats of music.

(2 counts) Repeat starting with the left foot. Keep feet in a toe-to-heel position throughout.

(4 counts) Repeat both sides again while moving forward.

(8 counts) Do four tarantella steps traveling backward.

Part 2: Face Partner

(8 counts) Tambourine moves using a triangle: Tap the left shoulder with the tambourine, do the same on the left and right hips. Repeat the triangle hitting the left shoulder, left hip, and right hip. Then, tap your left hand with the tambourine twice.

(8 counts) The man and the woman do a right shoulder do-si-do (that is, two tarantella steps forward passing right shoulders, then two tarantella steps backward passing left shoulders) and return to place.

(8 counts) Tambourine moves using double rhythm: Tap left shoulder with tambourine, tap right hip. Repeat to tap left shoulder and right hip. Then, tap left hand with tambourine twice.

(8 counts) Repeat the do-si-do.

Part 3: Man Kneels; Woman Circles

(16 counts) Man: Step with the left foot, kneel on the right knee. Continue to tap the tambourine on the right hip and the left hand until counts 7 and 8 (hit the tambourine twice). Continue kneeling for eight more counts. Woman: Perform in-place eight tarantella steps with both hands on hips.

(16 counts) Man: Remain kneeling, shaking the raised tambourine and looking at the woman. Woman: While shaking the raised tambourine, do eight forward tarantella steps in a counterclockwise circle around the man.

Part 4: Star Formations

(16 counts) All four dancers join right hands in the center to form a star and do eight tarantella steps in a clockwise circle. On the last count, clap the tambourine.

(16 counts) Turning about to join left hands in the center, do eight tarantella steps in the opposite direction. On the last count, clap the tambourine.

▶ Modifications

- Perform the dance without tambourines.
- Begin at a slow tempo and gradually increase speed.
- Learn the feet first, then the arms.
- Put the steps together in any combination—be creative!

▶ TRIVIA TIDBITS ◀

- Pinocchio is Italian for "pine eyes."
- From antiquity to modern times, Italy has played a central role in world culture. Italians have contributed some of the world's most admired sculpture, architecture, painting, literature, and music, particularly opera.

KOROBUSHKA
(kuh-rób-oosh-kah)

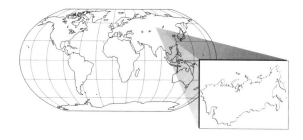

▶ Origin
Russia

▶ Location
Partly in Europe, Russia is bordered by the Arctic Ocean, China, and the Pacific Ocean.

▶ Language
Russian

▶ Flag
Three horizontal stripes of white, blue, and red

▶ Traditional Costume
Men wear shirts with full sleeves or tunics with embroidered designs, baggy pants to allow free movement, tall boots, and very long sashes that wrap around the waist several times and secured by tying. Women wear knee-length full dresses trimmed with colorful ribbons, tall boots, possibly scarves around the neck, and ribbons and/or flowers in the hair.

▶ History of Dance
This dance was developed by Russian immigrants after World War I on American soil. *Korobushka* translates as "little basket" or "peddler's pack." This dance style comes from the European part of Russia.

▶ Difficulty Level
Moderate

▶ Stance

Erect, with dignity

▶ Music Selection & Time Signature

Korobushka (4/4 time)

▶ Number of Participants

No limit of couples

▶ Formation

Double-circle partners with men on the inside circle and women on the outside circle, partners facing each other, man's back to center.

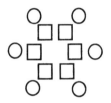

Directions

Part 1: Partners Begin Holding Both Hands

a. Three Walks and a Hop

(4 counts) The men step forward with a left, right, left, and hop on their left foot while the women step backward with a right, left, right, and hop on their right foot. Both partners move the hands in small circles during these steps.

(4 counts) Reverse directions to repeat the three walks and a hop. Men travel backward as they step right, left, right, and hop on the right foot. Women travel forward as they step left, right, left, and hop on the left foot.

(4 counts) Repeat three walks and a hop (forward for the men and backward for the women).

b. Cross, Side, Together

(4 counts) Men: Hop on the left foot and point the right toe diagonally in front of the left foot (to cross on count one). Women: Hop on the

right foot and point the left toe diagonally in front of the right foot (to cross on count one). Both hop and extend the pointed foot to the side (on count two). Both jump and bring feet together (land on count three), then hold on count four.

Part 2: Turn and Balance

a. Three Step Turn Away From, Then Toward Partner

(4 counts) Both partners take three steps to turn clockwise and clap on count four.

(4 counts) Both partners take three steps to turn counterclockwise and grasp right hands.

b. Balance and Trade Places

(2 counts) Partners step forward with the right foot and do a triple step (right, left, right).

(2 counts) Partners step backward with the left foot and do a triple step (left, right, left).

(4 counts) Partners walk forward to trade places and the man lifts his right hand to form an arch for the woman to turn counterclockwise, bringing her to his right side.

(16 counts) Repeat Part 2.

Continue to repeat from the beginning of the dance until the music stops.

▶ Modifications

- Practice each part without a partner, then with a partner.
- Substitute a grapevine step (side step, cross behind, side step) away from then toward partner during the three step turns (in Part 2a).
- Substitute a step and a touch for the triple step used in the balance forward and backward (in Part 2b).

▶ TRIVIA TIDBITS ◀

- The biggest bell in the world is the Tsar Kolokol, cast in the Kremlin in 1733. It weighes 216 tons, but it is cracked and has never been rung.
- The longest river in Europe, the Volga, is located in Russia.

GATHERING PEASCODS
(gath'-ahr'-ing pes'-kods)

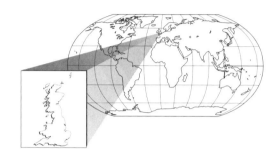

▶ Origin
England

▶ Location
Off the coast of western Europe, between the Atlantic Ocean and the North Sea

▶ Language
English

▶ Flag
Blue background, with the red cross of Saint George, edged in white, superimposed on the diagonal red cross of Saint Patrick, which is superimposed on the diagonal white cross of Saint Andrew. This design is also known as the Union Jack.

▶ Traditional Costume
(Late 16th century) The men wear peasant shirts, open vests, baggy pants or tights, tall socks, and shoes or boots. The women wear peasant blouses, long underskirts, overlayers of skirts, maybe a ring of flowers in their hair or unique hats, and flat shoes or boots.

▶ History of Dance
This dance was probably danced in celebration of the harvest. The English people of the Elizabethan era had very strong beliefs; all the circle dances started to the left, the "way of the sun," so as not to upset the gods.

▶ Difficulty Level
Moderate

▶ Stance
Somewhat erect, dignified

▶ Music Selection & Time Signature
Gathering Peascods (4/4 time)

▶ Number of Participants
Four to eight couples in each circle

▶ Formation
Partners in a single circle, with the woman on the man's right

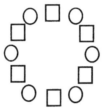

Directions

Verse 1: Sashay and Turn Single

(8 counts) Holding hands and moving clockwise, perform eight *sashays* (slides) to the left side.

(4 counts) Drop hands and turn single (individually turn by walking clockwise in a small circle).

(8 counts) Holding hands and moving counterclockwise, perform eight sashays to the right side.

(4 counts) Drop hands and turn single (individually turn by walking clockwise in a small circle).

Chorus: Alternating Inner Circles

(12 counts) The men form an inner circle, sashay clockwise, and return to starting position while the women stay in place.

(12 counts) The women form an inner circle, sashay clockwise, and return to starting position while the men stay in place.

(4 counts) The men take four walks forward to the center and clap hands on count 4.

(4 counts) The men walk four steps back to place, as the women take four walks forward to the center and clap on count 4.

(4 counts) The women take four walks back to place, as the men take four walks forward to the center and clap on count 4.

(4 counts) The men turn single to return to place, while the women stand in place.

(16 counts) Repeat the chorus, except that the women walk forward to the center first.

Verse 2: Siding and Turn Single

a. Siding Over and Back

(4 counts) Walk forward with left shoulder toward partner and exchange places

(4 counts) Walk forward with right shoulder toward partner and exchange places.

b. Turn Single

(4 counts) Turn single in place to the right.

(8 counts) Repeat siding over and back with your partner.

(4 counts) Repeat the turn single in place to the right.

Chorus: Alternating Inner Circles

(56 counts) Repeat the chorus.

Verse 3: Arming and Turn Single

(8 counts) Arm right as follows: Hook right elbows and walk around your partner.

(4 counts) Turn single in place to the right.

(8 counts) Arm left as follows: Hook left elbows and walk around your partner.

(4 counts) Turn single in place to the right.

Chorus: Alternating Inner Circles

(56 counts) Repeat chorus.

End with men bowing and women doing a curtsy to their partners.

▶ Modifications

- Use colors to distinguish between the inner and the outer circles; for example, add scarves, vests, or name tags in order to avoid confusion whenever there is an imbalance of males and females.
- Practice the first verse with the chorus until comfortable, then add the second verse, and so forth.

▶ TRIVIA TIDBITS ◀

- In England, the Speaker of the House is not allowed to speak.
- England is one of the few countries that still has a King or Queen as the chief figurehead.

TINIKLING
(tin-nik´-kling)

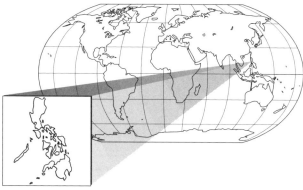

▶ Origin
Philippines

▶ Location
Southeastern Asia, between the Philippine Sea and the South China Sea

▶ Language
Tagalog is the traditional language. English and Spanish are both official languages.

▶ Flag
Two equal horizontal bands of blue and red with a white triangle on the left side. In the white triangle is a yellow sun with eight primary rays and in each corner is a small yellow five-pointed star.

▶ Traditional Costume
The men wear pants rolled up, *camisa de chino,* (cotton shirt; a t-shirt is acceptable), and a scarf tied around the neck. The women wear a colorful knee-length dress called a *Balintawak* costume. A scarf can drape over the shoulder. Usually no shoes are worn.

▶ History of Dance
This dance originated from Leyte island and depicts the flight of the *tikling* bird as it travels through the rice fields, avoiding bamboo traps

made by the farmers. The dancers weave in and out of the bamboo sticks trying not to get caught in the "traps." Bamboo sticks are also known as *tinikling* sticks and are required in this routine. Bamboo lengths must be at least 6 1/2 feet long. For safety purposes there should be two pieces of wood (1 1/2 inches thick and 2 feet long) placed under the poles (one on each side) in front of the clicker (the clicker is the person holding one end of the poles). Tinikling gets very acrobatic and rhythmic.

▶ Difficulty Level

Moderate/advanced

▶ Stance

Two clickers sit on their knees on the ground. Two dancers are standing.

Note: You need to slide *the bamboos together on the "close," as opposed to lifting, so that the dancers do not trip when the bamboo poles are lifted.*

▶ Music Selection & Time Signature

Tinikling (3/4 time)

▶ Number of Participants

Minimum of four

▶ Formation

Two clickers sit on their knees on the ground holding tinikling sticks (bamboo poles). Two dancers are standing. Clickers: On count 1, tap the poles on the floor. On count 2, tap the poles again on the floor. On count 3, slide the poles together to make a clicking sound. (Repeat this same pattern throughout the whole dance.)

Directions

In tinikling, there are eight figures, and each figure lasts 16 measures. Figures always begin on the left side of the bamboo from the dancer's point of view with the dancer's right shoulder closest to the poles.

Dancer's Basic Step

(1 count) Hop on the right foot in between the poles.

(1 count) Hop on the left foot in between the poles.

(1 count) Hop on the right foot outside of the poles (to dancer's right side) lifting the left foot in the air.

(3 counts) Repeat basic step, starting with the left foot.

Part 1: Basic Figure

(3 counts) Starting with the right foot, do the basic step. On the third count, raise the outside arm overhead and rotate the wrist inward (*kumintang*). Place the other hand behind your back.

(3 counts) Starting with the left foot, repeat the basic step, adding arm motions as just described.

(42 counts) Repeat Part 1 seven more times.

Part 2: Basic With Turn Figure

(3 counts) Starting with the right foot, do the basic step.

(3 counts) Turn a half turn to the right, then step backward three steps.

(42 counts) Repeat Part 2 seven more times.

Part 3: Heel and Toe Figure

(1 count) Touch the right heel in between poles.

(1 count) Touch the right toe in between poles.

(1 count) Hop over the poles onto the right foot.

(3 counts) Repeat the preceding three counts starting with the left foot.

(42 counts) Repeat Part 3 seven more times.

Part 4: Crossover Figure

a. Step, Hop, Cross

(1 count) Step on the right foot in between the poles.

(1 count) Hop on the right foot.

(1 count) Cross the left foot over the right foot and step to the outside of the poles (to dancer's right side).

b. Cross, Hop, Step

(1 count) Cross the right foot in front of the left foot and step in between the poles.

(1 count) Hop on the right foot.

(1 count) Step on the left foot outside of the poles (to dancer's left side).

(42 counts) Repeat Part 4 seven more times.

Part 5: Kuradang Figure

Note: This figure happens outside the bamboo poles. Arms are slowly moved out toward the sides, passing through first, second, third, and fourth ballet arm positions.

a. Step, Close, Step, Cross

(1 count) Step diagonally forward with the right foot. Arms are held in front of the chest.

("and" count) Close the left foot to the right foot.

(1 count) Step out with the right foot.

(1 count) Cross the left foot in front of the right foot.

b. Step, Close, Step, Point

(1 count) Step diagonally backward with the right foot.

("and" count) Close the left foot to the right foot.

(1 count) Step out with the right foot.

(1 count) Point the left toe forward in front of the right foot while the right hand goes overhead and performs *kumintang* (circular hand movement).

(6 counts) Repeat (a) and (b) except start with the left foot (left arm up by the ear on the point).

(36 counts) Repeat all of Part 5 three more times.

Part 6: Hopscotch Figure

(2 counts) Jump in between the poles on both feet twice.

(1 count) Jump outside of the poles on both feet, straddling the poles.

(45 counts) Part 6 repeats 15 more times.

Part 7: Crossover Variation Figure

a. Both Dancers Face the Same Way

(1count) Step on the right foot in between the poles.

(1 count) Hop on the right foot.

(1 count) Cross the left foot over the right foot and step to the outside of the poles (to dancer's right side).

(1 count) Step on the right foot in between the poles.

(1 count) Hop on the right foot.

(1 count) Cross the left foot back and step outside of the poles (to dancer's left side and starting position).

(6 counts) Repeat (a) above.

b. Add a Half Turn

(1 count) Step on the right foot in between the poles.

(1 count) Complete a half turn on the right foot in between the poles.

(1 count) Hop on the left foot outside of the poles (to the dancer's left side).

(1 count) Step on the right foot in between the poles.

(1 count) Hop on the right foot.

(1 count) Cross the left foot over to the outside of the poles (to dancer's right side).

(1 count) Step on the right foot in between the poles.

(1 count) Hop on the right foot.

(1 count) Step on the left foot outside of the poles (to dancer's left side).

(1 count) Step on the right foot in between poles.

(1 count) Complete a half turn on the right foot in between the poles.

(1 count) Step on the left foot outside the poles (to dancer's left side).

(24 counts) Repeat Part 7.

Part 8: Basic Step With a Partner

Note: This step is done with a partner. Both should be facing the same direction holding right hands at shoulder level and left hands palm to palm (by the left ear).

(3 counts) Starting with the right foot, do the basic step and raise the left arms overhead. (Raise the same arm as foot on count 3).

(3 counts) Starting with the left foot, do the basic step, raising right arms overhead.

(42 counts) Repeat Part 8 seven more times.

Ending

Partners bow or pose (clickers may lift one pole to form an "X").

▶ Modifications

- When first learning, perform the dance without the poles. Practice the footwork first, then add the arms.
- Decrease the tempo while learning and increase it when desirable.
- To simplify, shorten the number of figures.
- For variety, on the hopscotch figure, have partners hold hands.
- Add turns and formation changes to increase difficulty.

▶ TRIVIA TIDBITS ◀

- When the Spaniards discovered the islands, they named them after King Philip of Spain and the pines trees they saw on the islands.
- The flag of the Philippines is the only national flag that is flown differently during times of peace or war. The flag is flown with the blue band on top in times of peace and with the red band on top during wartime.

SIEGE OF ENNIS
(seeg of innis)

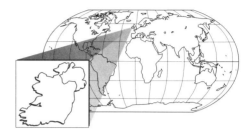

▶ Origin
Ireland

▶ Location
Western Europe. Ireland is an island in the Atlantic Ocean west of Great Britain.

▶ Language
English, Irish

▶ Flag
Three equal vertical bands of green, white, and orange

▶ Traditional Costume
In the 1800s the men wore hats, swallowtail coats, knee breeches, white stockings, and black shoes with silvery buckles. In the early part of this century older men adopted the kilt. Today, both kilts and pants are worn. Women of the 1800s wore peasant dresses (probably their Sunday best) and possibly a hooded cloak over a white dress with a sash. Embroidery on dresses was minimal in the 1800s, but today it is quite elaborate; the interlocking and continuous lines in the patterns symbolize the continuity of life and eternity.

▶ History of Dance
Ennis is a town in County Clare on the west side of Ireland. This dance represents the battle when Ennis was sieged. In the advance and retire (or retreat) portion of the dance one can imagine a battle taking place followed by a rearrangement of forces, a confrontation or struggle, then a moving on to begin again.

▶ Difficulty Level
Moderate/advanced

▶ Stance
Stand straight with arms at sides and chin up. When holding hands, hold lightly with hands at ear level. The steps are performed on the toes or ball of the foot. Feet are generally placed one in front of the other (crossed).

▶ Music Selection & Time Signature
Calliope House/Whelan's Jig/The Pipe on the Hob (6/8 time)

▶ Number of Participants
Minimum of four couples

▶ Formation
Two or more rows of four facing each other

Directions

Part 1: Promenade Step

Note: On all basics, maintain a heel-to-toe position (called fifth position in ballet) throughout the dance. Begin the dance with the right toe pointed.

a. Advance (Forward Two Basics)

(2 counts) Skip on the left foot and lift the right foot up beside the knee of the left foot (on "and" count). Step on the right foot, placing it in front of left foot on floor (on count 1). The left foot is moved into position behind the right foot, keeping most of the weight on the ball of the foot (on "and" count). Step forward on the right foot, taking a small step (on count 2). Thus, the advance combines a skip and a triple step (moving forward).

(2 counts) Skip on the right foot and do a triple step forward, stepping left, right, left.

b. Retire (Backward Two Basics)

(2 counts) Skip on the left foot (on "and" count) and lift the right foot up beside the knee of the left leg. Moving backward, place the right foot behind the left foot on floor (count 1). Step on the left foot,

keeping it in front of the right foot (on "and" count). Then step backward on the right foot, taking a small step (on count 2). Thus, the retire combines a skip and a triple (moving backward).

(2 counts) Skip on the right foot and do a triple step backward, stepping left, right, left.

(4 counts) Repeat the Advance.

(4 counts) Repeat the Retire.

Part 2: Side Step (Sevens)

Note: In the line of two couples, the couple on the right-hand side travel to the left and cross in front while the couple on the left-hand side travel to the right and cross behind.

a. Travel to Side

("and" count) Skip (lift right foot up at knee, and hop on the left foot).

(1 count) Step on the right foot, placed in front of and to the right of the left foot.

("and" count) Step on the left foot, placed behind the right foot.

(1 count) Step on the right foot, toward the right side.

("and" count) Step on the left foot, placed behind the right foot.

(1 count) Step on the right foot, toward the right side.

("and" count) Step on the left foot, placed behind the right foot.

b. Retire

(4 counts) Repeat (b) of Part 1, while staying in place.

c. Return to Place

("and" count) Skip: Lift the right foot up beside the knee of the left leg and hop on the left foot.

(1count) Moving backward, step on the right foot, placed behind the left foot.

("and" count) Step on the left foot toward the left side.

(1 count) Step on the right foot, placed behind the left

("and" count) Step on the left foot toward the left side.

(1 count) Step on the right foot, placed behind the left.

d. Retire

(4 counts) Beginning with the left foot up, skip backward two basics, while staying in place.

Part 3: Swing Around

(16 counts) Reach hands out to the person across from you, holding right hands on top of left hands. Using the Advance portion of the promenade step perform *only* eight skip-and-triple steps forward. Dance around each other clockwise approximately two revolutions and back into place, catch hands in the rows of four, and bring hands up above the shoulders.

Part 4: Advance and Retire

(8 counts) Rows A and B hold hands and advance and retire with the promenade step.

(8 counts) Dancers in lines pass through on the second time forward.

Part 5: Advance, Retire, and Arch Through

(8 counts) Rows A and B hold hands and Advance and Retire with the promenade step.

(8 counts) Rows A and C now make arches, and Rows B and D drop hands and pass through the arches, passing right shoulder to right shoulder while dancing the promenade step Advance only. Now, Rows A and D are facing each other ready to begin again, hence the term *progressive dance*.

▶ Modifications

- Decrease the tempo when first learning.
- Shorten the sequence by alternating Parts 1 and 3.

▶▶ TRIVIA TIDBITS ◀◀

- The correct response to the Irish greeting, "Top of the morning to you," is "and the rest of the day to yourself."
- The Blarney Stone is a stone in the Blarney Castel that millions of people have kissed to supposedly receive the gift of gab.

DUNANTULI UGROS
(doon'-ahn-tooli oo-grosh)

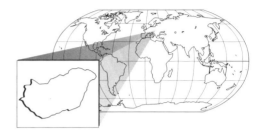

▶ Origin
Hungary

▶ Location
Central Eastern Europe, surrounded by Slovakia, Romania, Croatia, Serbia, and Austria

▶ Language
Hungarian

▶ Flag
Three equal horizontal stripes of red, white, and green

▶ Traditional Costume
Men wear jodhpur-type trousers with tall black riding boots, white dress shirt and a longer straight buttoned vest, and a hat. Women wear a full-sleeved jacket, knee-length skirt with petticoats and a decorated apron, and boots or black shoes.

▶ History of Dance
The *Duna* (Danube) river flows through Hungary, and to the east of it is a region called the *Dunantul*. This dance from the Dunantul is called a *ugros,* or jumping dance, because the steps to the dance are jumping steps.

   In Hungarian dance, partner dances are led by the men and are improvisational, meaning the steps are put together as the dance goes along. The steps that are shown can be put together in any order. The dance can be done with a partner or alone, but in Hungary most commonly men and women dance as couples.

The dances are characterized by high-spirited jumping figures and the use of everyday farm tools, such as herder's sticks, axes, and the *Karikas ostor,* or whip. Socially, these dances can be an expression of competition between the young men of the village, or between villages.

In Hungarian dance, rhythms are counted in series of beats called *ti* for short beats and *ta* for long beats. For example, the common phrase *ti-ti-ta* can be counted as *short-short-long.*

▶ Difficulty Level
Moderate/advanced

▶ Stance
Upright

▶ Music Selection & Time Signature
Dunantuli Music (4/4 time)

▶ Number of Participants
No limit

▶ Formation
Couples facing either in a line or a circle

Directions

Note: Both partners do the same step, starting on the same foot.

Part 1: Leap, Heel, Stomp (ti-ti-ta)

(2 counts) Start by grasping your partner's right hand in a handshake. The first step is leaping onto the right foot to the right side (a short "ti" on count 1). Then, dig the left heel (or use a flat-footed stomp) (a short "ti" on the & count). Then, step on the right foot, keeping it in place (a long "ta" on count two). The left foot is now free.

(2 counts) Repeat the preceding to the left starting on the left foot.

(28 counts) Repeat Part 1 seven more times.

Part 2: Lower-Leg Swing

a. Face Partner

(4 counts) Hop on the left foot, lift the right leg in the air, bend the knee at a 90-degree angle, and let the right heel swing away from the body

(on count &). Hop and swing the right foot across the left leg (on count 1), then swing the right foot back to the right (on count 2). Leap onto the right foot, dig the left heel, and stomp the right foot (repeating one side of the "ti-ti-ta" on counts 3-&-4. The left foot is now free.

(4 counts) Hop on the right foot, lift and bend the left knee 90 degrees to let the left heel swing away from the body (on count &). Swing the left foot across the right leg (on count 1), then swing the left foot back to the left (on count 2). Leap onto the left foot, dig the right heel, and stomp the left foot (again repeating one side of the "ti-ti-ta" on counts 3-&-4). The right foot is now free.

(8 counts) Repeat (a).

b. Move in a Circle

(24 counts) Repeat (a) while moving counterclockwise in a circle with your partner (still holding right hands).

Part 3: Double Heel Click in Air

a. Face Partner

(2 counts) Stand on both feet with feet parallel. Bend at the knees and jump into the air and land on both feet, keeping them approximately shoulder-width apart (on count 1). Push off to click the heels of your shoes together in the air (on count &). Land on both feet (shoulder-width apart) on count 2. Push off to again click the heels of your shoes together in the air (on count &).

(2 counts) Land on one foot and repeat one side of the "ti-ti-ta" on counts 3 & 4.

(48 counts) Repeat (a) 10 more times.

b. Change Places With Partner

(16 counts) Continue to repeat the double heel clicks in the air and change places with your partner by passing right shoulders (can hold either one or two hands with partner) on the "ti-ti-ta" portions.

Part 4: Ti-Ti-Ta Moving Counterclockwise

(4 counts) Face partner. Hop on the right leg, and point the left leg straight out in front of you with the toe on the ground (on count 1). Switch legs to hop on the left leg and point the right leg in front of you (on count 2). Then, repeat one side of the "ti-ti-ta" on counts 3 & 4 (modifying it slightly by crossing the left foot behind the right foot (on the & count).

(36 counts) Repeat Part 4 nine more times.

Part 5: Clapping Sequence for Men

Note: Men may do any number of repeats and need to give each action one count. Women may repeat any other part in any order as the men perform the various clapping sequences.

(4 counts) Slap the top of your leg as follows: Lift and kick the right leg straight in front of you and slap the top of your leg with your right hand (on count 1). Clap both hands together (on count 2). Lift and kick the left leg straight in front of you and slap the top of your leg with your left hand (on count 3). Clap both hands together (on count 4).

(4 counts) Lift the right leg sideways, slap right ankle, then clap the hands together. Lift left leg sideways, slap left ankle, then clap hands together.

(4 counts) Alternately clap hands under the lifted leg and in front. Repeat with the other leg.

▶ Modifications

- Start with multiples of 8 or 16 repetitions within each part in order to make the dance easier.

- Gradually add more and more parts until the entire dance is learned.
- Rotate counterclockwise with your partner while doing Part 3.
- In Part 5, add the following variations to the clapping sequence for the men: alternate an under-the-leg clap with a double clap in front; alternate an under-the-leg clap with a triple clap in front.

▶ TRIVIA TIDBITS ◀

- The stress in Hungarian words always falls on the first syllable.
- Hungarian folk music absorbed features of Oriental harmony from the Turks, who occupied the country in the 16th and 17th centuries.

Teaching multicultural folk dancing is an exciting adventure. You have an opportunity to meet all types of wonderful people and help them learn about themselves and each other through movement. Whether you are an experienced teacher or just getting started, here are some teaching techniques to assist you in your endeavors.

The essence of folk dancing is found in the spirit of each dancer and in the atmosphere that permeates the group. Thus, attention should be given to making the students feel comfortable and successful. A good educator should "feel" the group, which is an art in itself.

Suggestions for successful class formats include opening each class by sharing some information about the country. The history of the dance gives meaning and spirit to the instruction. For the first class, have students introduce themselves to each other. Teach a dance that does not require a partner, such as the Hora. Play the music a few times and have the class clap their hands to the beat. Increase the bass on the sound system if anyone is having trouble hearing the beat of the music. It is advisable to have a sound system with a speed control so you are able to increase and decrease the tempo of the music to adjust to the class environment.

Always play music, even if the volume is low. It is a great motivator and creates a feeling for the country. The body needs to be warmed up gradually, so have the dancers walk in place in time to the music. Then they can walk forward and back and side to side. After the first class, you can actually warm up the students by reviewing a dance they have already learned. Just remember to walk through the dance slowly and gradually increase the tempo.

Once you have warmed up the group, introduce the new dance. Begin by teaching the easiest moves to increase their self confidence. Review parts of the dance that may require more attention. Repeat the sections numerous times. Then teach the entire dance, paying special attention to correct terminology. If the dance is a circle dance, you may find it easier to teach it in a straight line first without having students hold hands. Be sure to tell students about the formation of the dance (circle, lines, squares, etc.), the direction of the dance (clockwise or counterclockwise) and which foot to start on.

The progressive method of teaching is a great technique. First, teach Part 1 of a selected dance. Once Part 1 is taught, have the students perform it first without the music, then with the music at a slow speed, and then increase the speed to the correct tempo. When they have performed Part 1 successfully, teach Part 2. After they have danced Part 2 successfully, add Part 1 and Part 2 together. Then teach Part 3. Continue on until all the parts are taught and the dance is completed.

Memorize your directions and calls. It is important for you to "cue" your dancers ahead of time. For example, on the 5th count of an 8 count, you can say, "Get ready to step right!" This takes practice, but is extremely helpful to the dancer. Make sure that you clarify when you are cueing the footwork (weight changes taken) or when you are cueing the beats of the music. For example, a triple step takes three weight changes within two beats of music. If the footwork actions are called out "1, 2, 3," then the students may think that this is the timing with the music when it is not.

When teaching moves that step side to side, turn and face the students and teach in opposition. A back to the audience is not as exciting as your smiling face, good projection, and enthusiasm. When teaching step patterns that move forward and back from the student, it is essential that you teach with your back toward them so they can follow your lead. When teaching partner dances, have partners face each other while you face your partner so you create a mirror image to the students before trying a dance formation. End each class with the students' choice of dance or with an old favorite. At the end of a high-energy dance, have the students walk around in a circle to cool down instead of abruptly stopping.

Some ideas for partner dances if you have more women than men (or vice versa) is to designate partners by other means. For example, give the "female" roles a color ("all the reds go over here") and give the "male" roles a different color. Maybe you can provide a colored arm band using ribbons or scarves. In addition, you can use gender-neutral terms to describe the different roles, for example, separate the dancers according to the formation (refer to the "inner circle dancers" and the "outer circle dancers") to avoid male/female gender references while teaching unequal groups. Challenge the dancers to perform a role versus "do the man's part (or the woman's part). While teaching dances that require a partner, it is always helpful to change partners frequently.

In planning a unit, keep in mind the students' ages, ability levels, the length of the class, and the number of lesson periods available. Every class will be different. Modify, modify, modify to fit your class! If *you* can't do it, chances are, *they* can't! Maybe you will get a class that is very coordinated and learns fast. Then you will need to challenge them by teaching faster, adding turns, and increasing tempo. The biggest test is when you have mixed ability levels in a class. A good solution to this situation is to teach to the beginning level and give the advanced dancers more advanced steps or modifications to perform during the same amount of time.

Always remember the main objective of folk dance is fun and fellowship. In dance everyone is a winner and students should feel very good about themselves. As a teacher, you can help create this feeling. Remember to have students warm up gradually and be sure to have them cool down correctly. Create images and cues that students' minds can adapt to easily. (Be sure to give the mind a "breather" before teaching a new step.) The students will feel good about themselves if they can successfully dance the progressions. They will feel comfortable around each other because of your positive teaching methods. All of this will create the atmosphere needed to let their spirits shine through and allow them to feel the real joy of multicultural folk dancing.

Dance Instructors (Volume 2)

Dulce Capadocia (Philippines)
Silayan Dance Company
316 N. Reno Street
Los Angeles, CA 90026
(213) 957-4778

Laura D'Angelo (Italy)
via G. Palumbo, 3
00195 (Roma) Italy
011-39-6-39734829

Alexandru David (Russia)
P.O. Box 139
Tarzana, CA 91356

Dawn L. Dyson (French Canadian)
Aman Folk Ensemble
P.O. Box 90593
Long Beach, CA 90809
(213) 661-5877

Lynnanne Hanson (England)
732 Brent Avenue
South Pasadena, CA 91030
(626) 441-0260

Hiroko Hojo (Japan)
200 S. Clark Drive
Beverly Hills, CA 90211

Athan Karras (Greece)
19300 Palomar Place
Tarzana, CA 91356
(818) 609-1386

Christy Lane
Christy Lane Enterprises
P.O. Box 4040
Palm Springs, CA 92263-4040
(800) 555-0205

Susan A. C. Langhout
P.O. Box 606
Bemidjio, MN 56619
(218) 755-2941

Michelle Larson (Ireland)
Larson Academy of Traditional Irish Dance
16339 Rutherglen Street
Whittier, CA 90603
(562) 947-7707

Janos Olah (Hungary)
Hungarian Folk Ensemble
640 South Exeter Place
Orange, CA 92869
(714) 639-9466

Equipment

For tambourines, hula skirts, Hawaiian leis, tinikling sticks, sombreros, and country flags, contact

Christy Lane Enterprises
P.O. Box 4040
Palm Springs, CA 92263-4040
(800) 555-0205

Complete your set!

Other items in the *Multicultural Folk Dance Treasure Chest*

Join Christy Lane as she shares the excitement and adventure of authentic dances from around the world.

Each dance on the **Multicultural Folk Dance Videos** is taught by a native of the country from which the dance originated or by an expert in that particular dance form. Wearing traditional costumes, these instructors show you step-by-step how to perform the dances. Then, a group of dancers demonstrates each dance in its entirety.

The **Multicultural Folk Dance Compact Discs and Audiocassettes** contain music derived from original, authentic compositions of the popular songs. Featuring the songs on the videos, the CDs and audiocassettes boast superior quality recordings, allowing you to hear and appreciate the traditional instruments.

The **Multicultural Folk Dance Guides** provide the following information for each dance: the country or region of its origin, the traditional costume of the dancers, a brief history of the dance, the difficulty level, stance and formation, directions for performing the dance, modification, trivia tidbits, and much more!

Multicultural Folk Dance Video — Volume 1 — Hosted by Christy Lane — HUMAN KINETICS VIDEO

Multicultural Folk Dance Compact Disc — Volume 1

Multicultural Folk Dance Guide — Volume 1

Multicultural Folk Dance Audiocassette — Volume 1 — Christy Lane, Susan Langhout

Volume 1 includes dances and songs from
- Israel
- Germany
- Mexico
- Hawaii
- Ghana
- Serbia
- Romania
- United States
- China

Volume 2 includes dances and songs from
- Greece
- Japan
- Canada
- Italy
- Russia
- England
- Philippines
- Ireland
- Hungary

For more information or to purchase the complete *Treasure Chest*, individual volumes, or single components, U.S. customers **call toll-free 1-800-747-4457**. Customers outside the U.S. use the appropriate telephone number/address shown in the front of this book